Hope

W9-APC-379

DISCARDED

BIRDS AND THEIR WORLD

THERE are thousands of kinds, or species, of birds. Some are so small that they look like insects; others, such as ostriches, weigh as much as two hundred pounds. Some fly or swim but cannot walk, and others that can walk and run are not able to fly.

Birds and Their World introduces us to birds of these and other kinds, and tells about the lives they lead. We meet robins that sing in backyards, grebes whose nests float on water, and warblers that make their homes in thick forests. We find that some birds prefer to live in cities and towns, though others like seacoasts, deserts, or lakes. Some stay in one region all through the year, but others travel to the South every autumn and come back in the spring.

Each aspect of bird life is introduced by a story about some familiar species. This story brings the subject to life—the life of one particular bird which almost anyone may watch. The story then leads to a discussion which tells what the subject means to birds in general. Illustrations show typical birds, their nests, their eggs, and the ways in which they live. The pictures also will help readers of eight to fifteen identify many of the birds to be seen near their homes.

Miss Pallas is a young naturalist who has had charge of the bird-of-the-month program of the New Jersey Audubon Society. Dr. Fenton is widely known as an author and illustrator, and as science consultant for the magazine *Children's Activities*. He published his first article on birds when he was sixteen; since that time he has watched birds in many parts of the United States, Canada, and Mexico.

Books by Carroll Lane Fenton

LIFE LONG AGO: THE STORY OF FOSSILS

ALONG THE HILL

EARTH'S ADVENTURES:
The Story of Geology for Young People

ALONG NATURE'S HIGHWAY

WEEJACK AND HIS NEIGHBORS

WILD FOLK AT THE POND

WILD FOLK IN THE WOODS

PREHISTORIC WORLD

By Carroll Lane Fenton and Mildred Adams Fenton

WORLDS IN THE SKY

RICHES FROM THE EARTH

By Carroll Lane Fenton and Dorothy Constance Pallas

BIRDS AND THEIR WORLD

Birds and Their World

By CARROLL LANE FENTON
and DOROTHY CONSTANCE PALLAS

Illustrated by Carroll Lane Fenton

The John Day Company   New York

598
F

Contents

Mig Robin sat on the ground and begged for food after he left the nest.

Robins and How Birds Fly

MIG Robin hatched from a greenish blue egg on a rainy day in May. He was a homely little bird with a very large beak and tightly closed eyes. There were wisps of gray down on his head and wings, but the rest of his body was bare. Mother Robin had to sit on the nest and cover him, for the weather was wet and chilly. Her feathers and the heat of her body kept Mig warm and dry.

There were three other eggs in the nest, and they hatched the very next day. Out came baby birds, or nestlings, that looked exactly like Mig.

The old robins had a busy time taking care of their young ones, which could not care for themselves. Father and Mother Robin caught caterpillars and soft-bodied insects on plants, and pulled squirming earthworms out of the ground. The old birds ate almost none of this food, but took it home and put it into the nestlings' mouths. At night and on chilly days, Mother Robin also had to sit on the nest and cover her little ones to warm them. On bright days she sometimes sat on the nest to keep the sunshine from making the babies too hot.

With such good care and so much food, the nestlings grew

7

and changed very rapidly. Spots on their skin became lumps. Then, after four or five days, the lumps began to turn into feathers.

Mig's new feathers did not look like those that covered Father and Mother Robin. They were rolled up tightly in thin tubes that ended in points, which explains why we call them *pin* feathers. Wisps of down clung to the points of the first pin feathers, giving the babies a worn, ragged look.

Next the pointed tubes began to split, letting the feathers inside them spread out. More feathers also grew on the young birds' backs and breasts, on their tails, on the sides of their heads, and on their wings. At first the feathers showed only in special places called *feather tracts,* with bare skin between. Later, when the feathers grew longer and spread out still more, they covered the bare patches.

While these changes were going on, Mig and his sisters opened their eyes. They also grew strong enough to stand up, flap their wings, and climb to the edge of the nest. By that time their feathers were long enough to form waterproof coats that completely covered them from their heads to their stubby gray tails. Their backs, wings, and heads were dark brownish gray, with whitish streaks on the wings and a white line around each eye. Their grayish white breasts had rusty red patches and were spotted with black. Those spots made the nestlings look like their relatives, the thrushes, not like grownup robins.

On the morning when Mig was two weeks old, he scrambled out of the nest and perched on a branch beside it. Soon he began to flap his wings, and then he let go of the branch. But instead

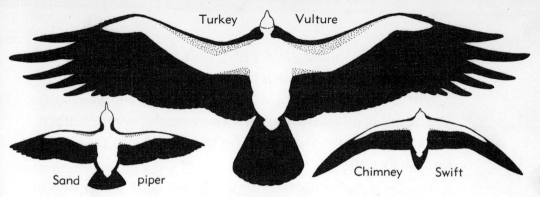

Turkey   Vulture

Sand   piper   Chimney   Swift

The black parts show how much feathers add to the wings and tails of three birds.

of flying away through the air, he fluttered down to the ground. There he sat and chirped loudly. He made so much noise that Father Robin hurried to him and gave him a juicy cutworm. As soon as Mig swallowed it he began to chirp again.

Mig's three sisters left the nest the next day. They sat on the ground, as Mig had done, and begged loudly for food.

In a few days the young robins became strong enough to sit up straight, run about, and even flutter into bushes. But they still wanted Father Robin to feed them, just as if they were small.

. . . . .

People often say that young birds "learn" to fly when they flutter out of their nests. Other people say that old birds "teach" their babies to use their wings.

Young birds really fly without learning or being taught. They move their wings up and down, and when they become big enough and strong enough the nestlings begin to fly. They do not learn to do so, as we learn lessons, and their fathers and mothers do not show them how to use their wings. But the

9

young ones do imitate, or act like, their parents, who also call encouragement to little birds that seem afraid to fly.

Still, flying is not so simple that it can be done any which-way. It depends upon several things, such as weight, wings, feathers, shape, and muscles. All these have to be just right in order for birds to fly well.

Weight is very important in flying, for light things stay in the air more easily than things that are heavy. Birds are built very lightly, with empty spaces called *air sacs* in their bodies. The large bones in their legs and wings are hollow, too, and other bones have shapes that make them strong although they are not heavy. Full-grown robins weigh just a few ounces, and eagles (which are very large birds) weigh only eleven or twelve pounds.

All birds that fly do so with their wings, but some wings are better than others. The best ones are much longer and wider than the body. They are big enough to carry the birds through the air swiftly for many, many miles.

Feathers give birds their streamlined shapes and air sacs make their bodies light.

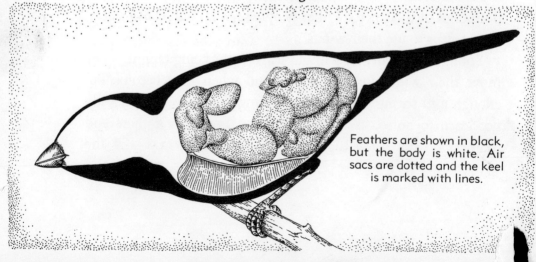

Feathers are shown in black, but the body is white. Air sacs are dotted and the keel is marked with lines.

All birds that fly have shapes that help them go through the air. Fairy stories and legends tell of horses, lions, and even bulls that had wings and were able to fly. Actually, none of these animals is shaped to "cut" the air, or go through it easily. But the bodies of birds are streamlined, which means that they taper smoothly from beak to tail. They remind us of airplanes, which also are streamlined.

Wings need strong muscles to lift even bodies that are not heavy and take them through the air. The muscles that move a bird's wings are fastened to a breast bone, or *keel,* on the underside of the body. Since the keel is very wide, the muscles that are fastened to it can be large and strong.

Feathers help birds fly in two ways. First, they make the wings so large they can lift the body, and so thin they can easily move through the air. Second, feathers form a smooth covering over the body. This covering, not the body itself, is what makes a bird truly streamlined.

.   .   .   .

There are several kinds of feathers. The two that are most important are *contour feathers* and *down.*

A contour is an outline. Contour feathers cover the heads, bodies, wings, and tails of most birds, giving them streamlined shapes and different outlines. Each contour feather has a central stem, or *shaft,* with a hollow *quill* at the end that is fastened to the skin. Many feathers also have a bit of downlike fluff where the shaft and quill come together. Branching off each side of the shaft are rows of strips called *barbs,* lying side by side so close together that they seem to form a single thin sheet, called the *vane.*

The barbs have side branches with tiny hooks and hold to each other almost like the parts of a zipper. If some barbs become separated, the bird smoothes them out with his beak and "zips" them up again.

Some contour feathers are soft and fluffy, but others are stiff, wide, and long. The widest ones are in the tail, but the longest and strongest are found in the wings. These flying feathers can lie flat, with overlapping edges, or they can turn sidewise and let the wing open almost like a Venetian blind.

Down feathers begin with short, hollow quills that are in the skin. Then comes a bunch of fluffy barbs whose side branches do not have hooks. Some down feathers grow on young birds, but others form a soft layer under the contour feathers of grown birds. If you see ducks swimming in icy water, you may be sure that thick layers of down are keeping their bodies warm.

Three kinds of feathers and their parts.

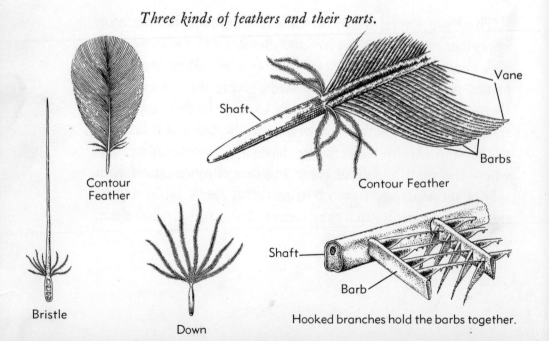

Contour Feather

Bristle

Down

Shaft

Vane

Barbs

Contour Feather

Shaft

Barb

Hooked branches hold the barbs together.

Some birds also have feathers which look so much like hairs that we call them bristles. A bristle has a short quill, a few tiny barbs, and a very thin shaft. Bristles around the mouths of kingbirds and other flycatchers (page 92) help them capture insects.

Different kinds of birds fly in different ways. Robins move their wings up and down at a regular rate. Woodpeckers beat their wings rapidly several times and then close them for a moment. Birds such as bobwhites, which have short rounded wings, beat them rapidly but soon stop and glide to the ground. Birds that have long wings, such as vultures and eagles, soar and glide long distances without beating their wings.

Suppose we watch a vulture soar. First he flies till he finds a place where air is rising from the ground in a current that blows upward for hundreds or thousands of feet. There the vulture begins to go in a circle, tilting the feathers in his wings so the air will take him upward. Soon he is so high that he looks like a dot in the sky.

The vulture may soar for a long, long time, or he may begin to glide. He does this by swinging away from the air current that has carried him upward. Then he holds his wings out straight and begins to slide downhill with the air. Down, down he goes, until he comes close to the ground. At last he flaps his wings and starts upward again, or finds an air current that is strong enough to lift him. He will keep on soaring, gliding and soaring again until he sees something to eat. When he does, he will glide down, flap his wings to stop, and alight on the ground or on his food.

13

Mother Starling built her nest in the hollow branch of an apple tree.

Nestlings, Beaks, and Food

MOTHER Starling built her nest in the hollow branch of an old apple tree. In the next week, she laid five pale blue eggs that hatched soon after the first day of May. The little birds were as wrinkled as Mig Robin and his sisters, but they had more down on their skins.

Sturnus Starling was the first little bird to hatch, and the first one to ask for food. He opened his mouth very wide and made a buzzing sound that seemed to mean "Feed me!" Father Starling brought a plump white grub, put it into Sturnus' mouth, and then pushed it down his throat.

Soon all five young starlings were buzzing and asking for food. They kept their parents busy from morning to night. The old birds found grubs, caterpillars, and soft-bodied insects and brought them home to the young ones. One day the starling parents made five hundred trips to find food, and five hundred trips back to the nest with the things they had caught.

Sometimes there was plenty of food for all five nestlings, but sometimes there was only enough for two or three. When that happened, Sturnus did not wait for his turn. He tried to get something every time, even though his stomach was full. Once, when Sturnus opened his mouth for a grub, he already had so much food that he could not swallow it. Mother Starling saw that the grub stayed in his throat, so she took it out and gave it to another nestling.

The babies called for food all the time until they were three or four days old. By that time they were able to tell when their father and mother were coming, and when they were far away. The nestlings began to beg only when their parents came to the apple tree.

After two weeks of eating and resting, Sturnus felt strong enough to scramble about in the nest and even to peek out of the door. By that time he was almost as large as his parents, and was covered with dark brown feathers. He also could eat many kinds of food. He liked hard-shelled beetles and crickets as well as soft-bodied grubs. He also swallowed crumbs, scraps of meat, and other things which his parents found beside a house at one end of the orchard.

One morning Sturnus scrambled so hard that he climbed out of the nest. He perched in the doorway for a few minutes and then fluttered down to the ground. There he sat without making a sound while his parents were away. But when they came with food, Sturnus fluttered toward them and begged loudly.

Although Sturnus seemed to be very hungry, he did not try
to feed himself. He followed his father and mother instead,
opening his mouth wide so they could put food into it. If something fell out, Sturnus fluttered and begged till one of his parents
picked it up and gave it to him again.

A day or two after Sturnus left the nest, he began to take
food from the beaks of his parents. Then he started to pick up
beetles and grubs. At last he stopped begging for food from
his parents and took care of himself. He made friends with several other young starlings that lived together in a flock. The
young birds went to another part of the orchard, and then flew
to a pasture where cattle grazed every day. The starlings walked
behind the cattle, catching insects that ran or hopped away from
their hoofs. The birds also poked their beaks down into the
grass and opened them as wide as they could. This pushed the
grass apart so the starlings could find grubs and beetles that
were hiding on the ground.

Young starlings are brownish and do not look like their par-

Birds that eat different foods have different beaks.

Hummingbird

Pelican

Sparrow

Golden
Eagle

Woodpecker

Whippoorwill

ents, which have shiny black feathers that glow with green and purple in the spring but are speckled with brown and cream-colored dots in the winter. Still, two things are the same in all starlings, whether they are young or grown-up. They have short tails and long, sharp beaks that are dark during most of the year but turn bright yellow in the spring.

. . . .

Birds that feed in different ways have beaks of different kinds. The pelican, for example, has a large beak with a pouch of skin on the underside. A pelican opens its mouth, plunges into water, and uses its beak as a scoop to catch fish. Then, when the young birds become hungry, the mother fills the back of her pouch with partly digested food. The babies reach in and eat it instead of trying to swallow fresh fish.

Sparrows, cardinals, and canaries eat hard seeds, not fish. These birds have thick, strong beaks that are just right for cracking such food. But hawks and eagles eat meat or fish, and their sharp, hooked beaks can be used to tear flesh into pieces. Ducks that eat plants and small animals have beaks that shovel up their food. Woodpeckers have beaks that are sharp and are flattened like chisels. The birds drive their chisel-shaped beaks into wood and catch grubs with tongues that are like small spears. But hummingbirds' beaks are long and slender, and are used to get sweet juice or little insects from long, cone-shaped flowers. Nighthawks have tiny beaks but very big mouths which can swallow insects as the birds fly through the air.

When a bird swallows food it goes down a tube called the *esophagus* (ee sof' uh gus), which runs from the mouth to the

17

stomach. The lower part of this tube is often widened into a pocket called the *crop,* in which extra food can be stored before it goes to the stomach. Some crops soften food and partly digest it, but others are just storage pockets. When ducks have had a big meal, you can see how their crops bulge with food.

After food goes through the esophagus it comes to the stomach. Birds that eat meat and insects have stomachs that soften food and digest it by means of chemicals. But seed-eating birds have stomachs that also grind their food into small bits.

A grinding stomach is called a *gizzard;* you can see one the next time your mother cooks a chicken. A gizzard looks rather like a purse, with thick sides that are made of strong, dark muscles. A bird whose stomach is a gizzard swallows small pebbles and sand as well as food. When the muscles squeeze the food this way and that, the pebbles grind hard seeds into particles as fine as flour.

After food is ground to pieces or softened it goes into the intestine, which is another long tube. Digested food soaks through the sides of the tube and into the blood, which carries it throughout the body. Part of the food becomes flesh,

An imaginary X-ray picture of a rooster showing his crop, gizzard, and some other organs.

skin, feathers, bones, and all the other things that make up the body of a bird. The rest of the food is used to produce energy that keeps the bird warm. Energy from food also is used to fly, find food, build nests, sing, and do other jobs of living.

Have you ever wondered why birds eat a great deal of food, even after they have stopped growing? They do so because they live at a faster rate than most other creatures, and therefore must turn more food into energy. A bird's body and blood are much warmer than yours, and its heart beats faster. It breathes more rapidly, too, and it may fly much faster than you can walk or run. Starlings, which beat their wings rapidly, can fly thirty to forty miles in an hour, or a mile in one and a half to two minutes. Wild geese can go faster than that, and the swifts that build nests in chimneys sometimes fly at the rate of eighty miles per hour.

If you want to realize how fast birds live, watch some robins or starlings that are taking care of their young ones. Notice how the mother keeps the little ones warm with her own body until the sun heats the air. Then watch the old birds hop about in search of worms and insects and fly to the nest with them as soon as they have a mouthful. If a cat or squirrel comes near they may drive it away by screaming and pecking, and by beating it with their wings. Then back they go to hunt grubs and caterpillars. You can't work as long and as hard as they do, or move as rapidly. Do you wonder that they use a great deal of energy and eat a great deal of food?

Chuck Catbird bringing grass for the nest which his mate built.

Finding Homes and Mates

ONE spring night a flock of catbirds came from their winter home in the South. They flew over woods, pastures, and fields until they came to a town. By that time the birds were tired, so they stopped to rest among some bushes. They perched in the bushes and slept till morning.

Chuck Catbird woke up and looked about as soon as the sky grew light. He found he was in his last-year's home, where he had hatched and grown up. He knew the bushes and the grape arbor that stood behind a house. He knew a tall pine tree and a bird bath, too, and a shelf where people who lived in the house kept food for different kinds of birds. They put out seeds and cracked grain for sparrows, but birds that liked to eat insects and berries got raisins and peanut butter.

Chuck soon flew to the shelf, but found only seeds and two

20

or three raisins. He ate them and went back to hunt insects in the bushes. Then he picked up several grubs.

The other catbirds spent the day feeding among bushes and flower beds, and in gardens. When night came the flock flew northward, but Chuck stayed where he was. Since this place was his summer home, he did not go on with the other catbirds.

Chuck spent the next three or four days deciding which bushes and trees, and just how much lawn, should belong to him. When a bird picks out his home ground in this way, we say that he chooses his *territory*. Chuck chose his territory and marked it for his own by singing at its edges, or boundaries. He sang in the pine tree, on a maple, and at both ends of the row of bushes. Although his songs had no words, they told other birds that all the ground between those places belonged especially to Chuck.

Other male catbirds also came to the town and chose their territories. One bird picked out a lawn with trees and bushes, right next to the place selected by Chuck.

This new catbird never tried to claim the central part of Chuck's territory, but he was not so careful near the boundaries. Chuck was sure that he owned the bird bath. Still, it stood so close to the other catbird's ground that he some-

Chuck often sang to his mate.

times acted as if it were his. When he did that, Chuck chattered angrily and chased him away.

The other catbird generally went without fighting, as if he knew that the bath really belonged to Chuck. But when they got to the other bird's territory he turned and drove Chuck back to the bath or to one of his own bushes. Each bird seemed to feel strong and brave in his own territory. Outside it he became timid, and was easily driven away.

. . . . .

One night a flock of female, or mother, catbirds stopped to rest in the town. When morning came most of them flitted away, but one stayed. Soon she began to hunt insects among the bushes and flower beds in Chuck's territory.

Chuck watched Lady Catbird for a few minutes and then flew down beside her. They hunted insects for a while and went to the bird bath, where Lady Catbird splashed and smoothed her feathers. Next they flew to the feeding shelf and then back to the bushes.

Chuck followed Lady Catbird for several days. Sometimes he perched beside her and sang soft songs. At other times he chased her, slipping and sidling through the bushes in what seemed to be a game of tag.

One morning Chuck flew down beside Lady Catbird as she perched in the maple tree. He fluffed the feathers on his breast, let his tail droop, and bowed. Then he said "Ma-aa!" and opened his beak very wide, showing a bright green leaf. Since she paid no attention, he dropped the leaf and began to chase her. They went round the maple, over the lawn, and into the bushes. There Lady Catbird let him perch beside her. This seemed to be her way of saying "I will be your mate."

Next day the two catbirds began to build their nest in a bush, about four feet above the ground. First they made a coarse basket of twigs, weed stems, and grass. Then they lined the basket with rootlets and strips of bark. Lady Catbird did most of the work, though Chuck often brought material and gave it to her. He also sang to keep other birds out of his territory. He sang in the evening as well as the morning, and sometimes kept on singing until the sky drew dark.

· · · · ·

Almost all birds have territories, but they are not alike. A catbird's territory is big enough to provide food for the father bird, his mate and their young ones. The same is true of a robin's territory, or an eagle's. Since eagles need a great deal of food in the form of fish or beasts, such as ground squirrels and rabbits, the home territory of an eagle covers several square miles.

Herons, gulls and other water birds go away from home to hunt food, and their territories are only large enough for their nests. Several herons sometimes nest in one grove or even one tree, and hundreds or thousands of sea birds nest on a single cliff. They don't seem to mind close neighbors, but

A snowy egret making its display.

they fight with birds that try to take the small amount of space which they need for their nests.

When male birds are choosing territory or trying to get mates, they often show off their feathers and even dance before females. This is called *display*. Chuck displayed his gray feathers to Lady Catbird, and the male robin displays the reddish feathers on his breast by fluffing them when he chooses his territory. This and his songs tell other male robins to stay away from the place he has chosen for his home.

Snowy egrets make very beautiful displays. These egrets are small white herons with black beaks, black legs, and yellow feet, and they live near the Gulf of Mexico. Some of their feathers, called plumes, are very long and fine. When an egret displays, it raises the plumes on its head, its back, and its breast until they look like white veils. Male and female egrets display to each other, even after their young ones hatch.

Ruffed grouse, which are sometimes called partridges, have two kinds of displays. A male grouse that wants a mate stands

This ruffed grouse is spreading his tail and ruff because another male has come near.

on a stone or log and spreads a ruff, or collar, of feathers on his neck. Then he leans back and beats his wings as fast as he can. They make a dull drumming sound which warns other males to stay away but attracts any female grouse that hears it. When a female comes near a male he smoothes his feathers and walks toward her. He picks at leaves and twigs as he goes, and then taps her beak. That seems to be his way of saying that he wants her for his mate.

A grouse that has drummed makes a very different display when another male comes into his territory. The drummer draws his head back into his ruff, lets his wings droop, and spreads his tail like a fan. Then he struts forward angrily, making a noise that sounds like *Sh-sussh!* When the other male hears this he may run away, or he may stand up angrily and fight. The two birds jump and peck, and beat one another with their wings. The one that loses the fight is driven away, and the one that wins keeps the territory. Of course, the grouse that drums and displays usually wins. This means that he keeps the territory that was his before the fight.

Mother Thrasher coming to her nest in the bushes.

Nests, Eggs, and Baby Birds

TWO brown thrashers decided to build their nest in some bushes beside a fence. They might have chosen a place on the ground, but Mother Thrasher liked a low, thick bush that was partly covered with vines. She brought dead twigs and laid them crisscross to make. the framework for her nest.

Both birds brought still more twigs and wove them into the framework. Then Mother Thrasher sat down in the center of the sticks, fluffed out her feathers, and moved to and fro. This pushed the twigs about until they formed a loose, rough basket. Many other birds also shape their nests to fit their bodies just as Mother Thrasher did.

As soon as the basket of sticks was built, the thrashers added dead leaves, grass, and strips of bark which they pulled from grape vines. Then came tiny twigs and a lining of roots. Mother

26

Thrasher sat on the nest many times, pushing it into shape. In the end it fitted her body, though her tail had to stick out over the rough edge.

Nest-building kept Mother Thrasher busy for four or five days, but Father Thrasher did not work so hard. He often perched on a branch and sang while his mate hunted twigs, and he drove catbirds or other thrashers away when they came into his territory. Still, he worked harder than male orioles, robins, or hummingbirds. Male hummingbirds do no nest-building, while robins and orioles do very little. Even when they bring twigs, grass, or other materials, their mates almost never use them.

On the morning after the nest was completed, Mother Thrasher sat on it for a half hour. She laid a pale blue egg that was spotted with brown. Then she slipped away to eat her breakfast of grubs and full-grown insects.

Mother Thrasher laid another egg each morning for the next three days. After the last egg was laid she fluffed her feathers, settled down, and sat in the nest for several hours. When she finally went away to eat, Father Thrasher sat on the eggs until she came back.

A bird that sits on its eggs is said to be *incubating* (in" kyu bay' ting). This means that the parent bird's body and feathers keep the eggs warm, so that young ones can grow inside the shells. In some kinds, or species, of birds, both the father and mother incubate, but in others only the mother does so. A few kinds—just a few—do not incubate at all.

Cowbirds do not incubate because they lay their eggs in other birds' nests. These other birds warm the eggs and take care of the cowbirds' young ones.

Brush turkeys, which live in Australia and on nearby islands, keep their eggs warm in a different way. The mother birds pile up mounds of fallen leaves and lay their eggs in them. As the leaves rot, or decay, heat is produced, and this makes the eggs develop. When they hatch, out come young birds that are able to run about on the ground and pick up their own food.

Day after day the thrashers took turns at incubating their eggs. Mother Thrasher also turned them over with her beak every morning and afternoon. This let the eggs become warm on all sides, so the little birds that were growing inside them could develop properly.

Thirteen days after the last egg was laid, the first one began to hatch. By that time the baby filled the whole shell and was strong enough to move about. It twisted and turned several times and then pecked a hole in the shell. The baby did this with a hard point called the *egg tooth,* at the tip of its upper

Cowbirds lay their eggs in the nests of other birds. The female cowbird is dull brownish gray, but her mate has a black body.

beak. The tooth was good for nothing else, and would fall off after a few days.

The little thrasher did not hatch all at once, as a Jack-in-the-box pops out when the lid of its box is opened. The young bird rested after pecking the hole in the shell. Next the little one pecked and wriggled again, until the shell began to crack. Then came another rest and some kicks, which made the large end of the shell fall off. But the baby bird had to rest again before he could get out of the shell.

Pecking and wriggling and resting took a lot of time, and each baby thrasher had to do it for himself. More than a day went by before all four little ones finally got out of the eggs. As they hatched, the parent birds picked up the broken shells and carried them far away from the nest. No cat or red squirrel that found the eggshells could tell where the baby birds were.

· · · ·

All kinds of birds lay eggs, and most birds build nests to hold them. But each kind of bird has its own sort of nest, which may be very different from the nests of other kinds, or *species* (spee′ sheez).

The simplest nests are made by birds that lay their eggs on the ground. The killdeer, for example, scrapes out a saucer-shaped place and lines it with wisps of grass or with pebbles that look like the bird's spotted eggs. Terns make their saucers in sand near the edge of a sea or a lake and use little lining or none at all. Gannets like steep cliffs at the edge of the Atlantic Ocean. A gannet's nest is a little mound of seaweed and dirt, with a rim that keeps the one bluish white egg from rolling away.

Kingfishers dig holes, or tunnels, in steep banks and lay their eggs on the dirt floor. Orioles live in trees and fasten their nests to the ends of branches. The mother oriole gathers grass, horse-hair, strings, and strips of tough bark and weaves them into a bag that hangs downward. Winds swing the bag-shaped nest to and fro, but it is fastened so tightly that it does not fall.

Barn swallows once nested in caves or hollow trees, but they now use buildings. A barn swallow's nest is shaped like half of a cup. It is made of dried mud mixed with straws that help to make it strong. The mother swallow lines her nest with fine, soft grass and feathers.

The eggs of different birds vary almost as much as their nests. Some are little and some are big; some are almost round, but others are pointed at one end. They have white, blue, and greenish shells or are covered with spots and wriggly lines of brown and other colors. But, in spite of these differences, all eggs have the same parts and are formed in the same way.

Every bird's egg is produced in the body of a female, or

Ruffed grouse's nest in the woods.

Herring gull guarding
its nest on the ground.

Common tern's nest on a beach.

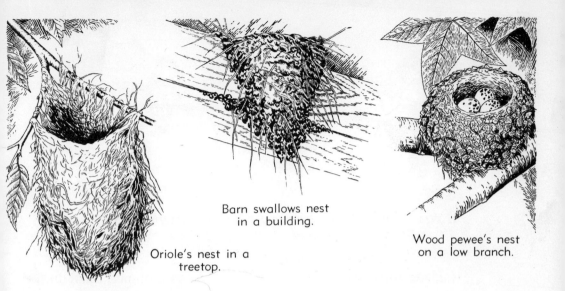

Barn swallows nest in a building.

Oriole's nest in a treetop.

Wood pewee's nest on a low branch.

mother. At first her eggs are very small, with no shell, no watery *white,* and almost no yellow, or *yolk.* These newly-formed eggs hang together in a cluster that looks like a bunch of very tiny cream-colored grapes.

When the mating, or nesting, season begins, some of these tiny eggs fill up with yolk. This makes them larger and larger, until they become yellow balls that separate from the cluster and go into the open end of a twisted tube that is part of the mother's body. Each ball has a dot that can grow into a baby bird after the mother mates.

When birds mate, tiny things called sperm cells come from the father's body and go into the mother's. One sperm cell can go into the dot on each egg, which begins to develop. This is called *fertilization,* and the egg becomes a *fertile* egg.

As the fertile egg goes through the tube, several important things happen. First the egg is covered with white, or *albumen*

31

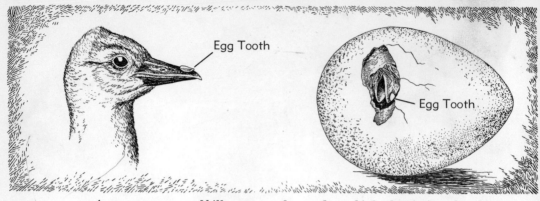

A very young sandhill crane and a turkey chick that is just hatching.

(al byu´ min). Next two thin "skins," or membranes, form and more watery albumen soaks through them. Then, as the egg keeps on going through the tube, a shell is made of hard, limy material. Last of all comes a thin coat that may be white, blue, or some other color. There may be dark markings, too, like those that make a killdeer's eggs resemble pebbles on the ground where the mother lays them.

If a fertilized egg grows cold, the living dot on the yolk soon dies. But when an egg is kept warm the dot becomes a baby bird which uses the yolk as food with which it can grow and develop.

At first the new bird inside the egg does not look like its parents or even like a nestling. It is just a tiny, soft creature with a big head and stubby bumps that can become legs and wings. But day by day the little creature changes. It develops eyes, skin, muscles, bones, and a beak with an egg tooth at the tip. At last it is big enough to hatch and to go on developing without being covered by a shell.

Eyes and Intelligence

HAL and his mate were called bald eagles, but their heads really were not bare, or bald. They were covered with short white feathers that seemed to gleam when the sun shone on them. The birds' tails were as white as their heads, but the rest of their feathers were dark brown.

The eagles made their home in a forest, far away from towns. There they built a nest of sticks on top of a tall, dead pine tree. They used the nest year after year. Each year they added more sticks to it, until it was more than eight feet wide and weighed about four thousand pounds.

When Hal and his mate perched near their nest, they could look down upon other trees in the forest. But when they soared they looked down upon valleys and ridge-shaped hills, and across a very large lake. On clear days they could even see the ocean, though it was many miles away.

Most birds have good eyesight, but the eagles' eyes are especially good. As Hal soared high up in the sky, he could see his mate when she was sitting on the nest. He could see rabbits on the ground, too, and could tell dead fish from white stones lying on the shore of the lake.

33

The eagles needed their good eyes as soon as their young ones hatched. The eaglets ate nothing except fish and meat, and their parents had to search all day in order to find food for them. They caught rabbits and ground-dwelling birds such as grouse. They picked up dead fish from the lake shore, and they took other fish from hawklike birds called ospreys. Sometimes the eagles also caught living fish. They seized the fish with their sharp-clawed feet, never with their beaks.

The eaglets ate a great deal and grew very fast, but they did not hurry away from the nest. They stayed in it almost three months before they finally flew away. By that time they were as big as their parents but their heads and tails were brown, not white.

Soon after the eaglets left the nest, Hal and his mate also went away for a summer trip. They flew northward two or three hundred miles to another lake. There they stayed for several weeks while they rested, fished, and flew together.

Eagles have three eyelids—an upper one, a lower one, and another at the side. This third eyelid is very thin and is almost clear, so the birds can see through it. When an eagle flies he often pulls this thin eyelid across the eye, keeping out wind and dust. Most other birds also have this third eyelid,

Hal, the bald eagle, could soar and glide for hours.

but those that seldom fly very far or very fast do not need it as much as eagles do.

As fall began, Hal and his mate came back to their regular home. There they stayed while most other birds went away to spend the winter in the South.

Early in February there was a terrible storm. Snow fell and wind blew so hard that people who lived near the forest could not go out of doors. Hal and his mate had to leave their nest and stay in living pine trees that sheltered them from the wind and snow.

When the storm ended, the eagles came back—but they could not find their nest or the tall, dead tree. The storm had blown it down, and the nest was only a pile of sticks lying on the ground.

Both eagles saw the fallen tree, but they did not know it was theirs. For two days they soared round and round, showing that they could not understand what had become of their nest. Then Hal's mate stopped looking for it, and began to carry sticks to the top of another pine tree. Soon Hal came to help her, breaking off branches and using them to build a new nest. It was not as big and heavy as the old one, but it was large enough for the eggs and the eaglets that would hatch from them.

· · · ·

We know that most birds have good eyesight, but they use their eyes in different ways. Owls, for example, have big eyes that get a lot of light and are very good for seeing at night. Owls also have their eyes at the front of their heads, just as human beings do. An owl can look straight forward when it is sitting

35

still and straight downward when it is flying. But a robin's eyes are at the side of its head, where they can look in most directions *except* straight forward. When a robin wants to look at something on the ground it has to turn its head sidewise and use only one eye. That is why robins seem to be listening when they really are looking for earthworms in the grass. Still, some scientists think the birds are able to hear worms as well as see them.

Eagles and hawks have their eyes near the front and can see things that are far away without turning their heads. Many hawks hunt for food by flying back and forth over meadows. The birds are hundreds of feet up in air, yet they see mice, grasshoppers, and even beetles on the ground below. But the woodcock's eyes are at the sides and near the top of its head. It can look at things above it and to the right and left. Some people say that the woodcock also sees things in front of it and behind.

We often think owls' eyes are very big, but all birds have eyes that are large in proportion to the size of their heads. Birds' eyes also contain rings of small, bony plates which strengthen them and protect them against the pressure of air.

Hawk

Mourning
Dove

Woodcock

Owl

The blue jay is one of the most intelligent birds.

Air pressure becomes very strong when a bird flies rapidly, often against the wind.

The eyes also are protected by skin and feathers that partly cover them, and by the third eyelid. Skin and feathers make a bird's eyes seem smaller than they really are.

Birds also have good-sized brains, but they are not used for the kind of thinking that human beings do. A bird's brain gets messages from its eyes, or "sees things," and does that very well. The brain also helps a bird keep its balance and controls the muscles used in flying. But it seldom has to think, for most of the things a bird does are done by *reflex* or *instinct*.

A reflex is something that is done quickly, without planning or thinking. Suppose you see a ball coming and dodge it; that is a reflex action. Birds use reflexes when they peck at food, fly away from cats, attack birds that come into their territories, and do many other things. When a bird hides "cleverly" in grass or bushes, it is only acting by reflex.

Instincts are more complex than reflexes. Instincts make birds able to build nests, to travel long distances, and to do various other things without learning how or "figuring them out." Each baby bird gets a set of instincts from its parents, and it passes them on to its own nestlings when it grows up and mates. That explains why every robin makes a nest of twigs, grass, and mud, and why orioles always put their bag-shaped nests at the ends of branches. When you watch birds you will see them do many things by instinct, and probably do them better than they would if they "figured things out."

Still, birds are able to think, and some do so much better than others. The jay is one of the best thinkers among our well-known birds. Jays quickly learn to eat strange food and get it from strange places. Jays also learn that some people hurt them and some do not, and they are able to count up to three. If three people hide behind a bush and one goes away, the jay knows that two others are still there. Many birds can count only to two, and others can count only one. If two people hide and one goes away, these birds act as if no one is left.

We often think that robins and other birds are intelligent because they come back to the same nesting place year after year. But they get into trouble when they leave the kind of nesting spots they always have used and try bridges or buildings. One pair of robins started five nests on five steps of a fire escape, and did not find out which was which till the female had laid several eggs.

A yellow warbler and a Maryland yellowthroat.

Kinds of Homes, or Habitats

A FLOCK of warblers came from the South on a rainy night in May. Since they did not like to fly in rain, they stopped among the trees and bushes that grew beside a creek.

When morning came the warblers were hungry. They hopped from branch to branch catching caterpillars, and they slipped through thorny bushes where full-grown insects were hiding. Now and then the birds called *Chip, cheep!* to each other or stopped to sing soft little songs.

The rain came to an end before noon, and most of the birds started northward again. They flew from bush to bush and from tree to tree, eating insects as they went. They would travel like that until night, but then they would leave the trees and go up into the air. There they would fly for several hours, till they found another good place to rest.

As the flock of warblers left the valley, one bird stayed behind. His full name was Dendroica (den dro' i ka). Since only scientists use it, suppose we call him Den.

Den was a yellow warbler, though people sometimes called him a wild canary. If they had looked at him closely, they would have seen that his beak was thin instead of thick, like the beak of a seed-eating canary. They also would have seen reddish streaks on Den's breast and sides and dull green on his back and wings. Some canaries have dull green backs and wings, but their breasts are not streaked with red.

Den's feathers had been washed by the rain, but he wanted to take a bath. His tub was a big saucer-shaped leaf that held a shallow pool of water. Den flitted through the pool several times, fluffing his feathers and shaking them. The large leaf shook too, and so did smaller leaves about it. Drops of water fell from them, giving Den a shower as well as a tub.

When Den finished his bath, he flew to the top of a willow tree and sat there preening himself. First he pulled each wing feather through his beak, pushing off drops of water and "zipping" the barbs together. Then he shook the feathers on his body and tail and arranged them neatly. Finally he rubbed them with oil from a pocket, or *gland,* in the skin near his tail. This oil made his feathers smooth and glossy. It also would keep them dry if rain began to fall again.

When night came Den perched in a wild blackberry bush. His thin toes curled around a stem and held it tightly. He put his head back over his shoulder, tucked his beak under the upper edge of one wing, and went to sleep.

The magnolia warbler builds its nest in open evergreen woods.

Other flocks of warblers flew northward while Den slept in the blackberry bush. Instead of singing the birds said *Chip-cheep!* over and over again. People who were awake at night heard them, but sleepy Den did not.

There were several kinds of birds in every one of these flocks. Some were yellow warblers like Den, but others called yellow-throats had bright yellow throats and black faces. Redstarts were black, salmon pink and orange, but magnolia warblers were gray, white, black and yellow, with black streaks on their yellow sides and breasts. Blackburnian warblers had orange and black on their heads and breasts. The orange was so bright that it seemed to shine, even on rainy days.

· · · · ·

All these warblers lived among bushes and trees, but they did not like the same kinds in the same sort of woodlands. This meant that whole flocks never stopped flying northward in a single place or region. Birds left the flocks one by one, when they came to the kinds of woods in which they wanted to live.

41

Some grebes have crests like these birds and some do not, but all build nests that float on the water.

Most of them also stayed near the places where they had hatched and grown up.

The place where Den left his flock was just right for yellow warblers. It had a creek and thick tangles of bushes, and most of its trees were small. For some reason yellow warblers never like to live among tall trees.

Maryland yellowthroats also liked bushy places, especially if they were swampy and had no large trees. Redstarts often rested in bushes while they were traveling northward, but they would not live among them. These birds wanted open woodlands or even lawns, where they could build their nests in young maples, oaks, and other trees with broad, thin leaves. Magnolia warblers liked open woods, too, but they nested in small spruces, firs, and hemlocks, which we call "evergreens." Blackburnian warblers kept on flying until they found woods where tall trees grew close together. The birds seemed to want shade, for they tucked their nests away in tall, thick spruce trees, firs, and pines.

42

We call each of these different woodlands a special *habitat* (hab' i tat). Actually, a habitat is any place where certain kinds of plants and animals live together. The plants may be little or big, and the animals may be anything from earthworms to fish, insects, birds or beasts.

Birds live in most of the habitats of shallow waters and on land. Grebes swim in lakes and ponds or along the seashore, and build nests that float in the water. Gulls, terns, and sandpipers also live near shores, but they make their nests on land. Golden eagles often live among mountains and nest on high cliffs, but burrowing owls dig holes in level plains or use holes dug by the animals known as prairie dogs. Other owls live in woods, which also are the homes of warblers, woodpeckers, and many other birds. Starlings prefer towns and cities, where they roost and even nest on houses and office buildings. A habitat with buildings, automobiles and electric lights seems to be just right for these noisy birds.

Col, the bobwhite, often looked for food under bushes and weeds.

Birds That Live on the Ground

WARBLERS live in bushes and trees, where some of them hunt insects on high twigs and branches. But Col hatched and grew up on the ground. Even when he flew he went only a few feet up into the air.

Col was the kind of quail called bobwhite, which lives in many parts of our country but is commonest in the South and East. He was a plump bird with reddish brown and white feathers that had many black and buff markings. He could raise the feathers on his head, but he did not have a black top-knot, like western quails.

Many bobwhites live in open forests or even in cities and towns. But Col made his home on a farm that had woods, a grassy pasture, and fields in which crops were grown. There were fences between some of the fields, and rows of bushes grew

44

beside the fences. The farmer would not cut down those bushy fencerows, for he knew that they made shelters and nesting places for birds.

When winter came Col and twenty other bobwhites lived in a flock, or *covey*. They slept in one of the fencerows, where they often ate seeds from last summer's weeds. The bobwhites also walked along their fencerow until they came to a cornfield. The ears of corn had been harvested, but many loose kernels had fallen to the ground. The bobwhites picked up those kernels and ate them. Since they were larger than weed seeds, they contained much more food.

The covey lived in the fencerow for several months, until spring began. Then the birds separated and went to different parts of the farm. Each male chose his territory and warned other males to stay away.

Col's territory was much larger than the territory of Chuck, the catbird. It contained part of a fencerow, one end of a field, and a corner of the woodland. These different places had different plants, as well as many kinds of insects. These things meant that there would be plenty of food from spring till the end of summer. There also was shelter from hawks, owls, cats, and other creatures that sometimes ate bobwhites.

After Col chose his territory, he wanted a mate to share it with him. He stood at the edge of the woods and called *Bob-bob-white?* in a whistling tone. He listened but no one answered, so he called again.

Col whistled many times as he walked at the edge of the woods. Then he went to the fencerow and called again. He did

45

not go to the field, for its plants had just begun to grow and still were small. Hawks could have found him easily if he had whistled in the field.

Just as Col started back toward the woods he heard an answer to his calls. The answer sounded like *A-loy, A-lee,* which meant that it was made by a female. Since the sound was faint Col knew that she was far away.

Col might have flown to the female bobwhite if she had been in his territory. Since she wasn't, he stood in his part of the fencerow and called *Bob-bob-white!* several times. Those calls would help the female find her way to him.

Soon Col heard a rustling sound—and there came the female. She was as big as Col and had the same shape, but her colors were not quite the same. He had a white throat and white stripe on each side of his head, but the feathers near these white marks were black. Her throat and head-stripes were buff, and the feathers near them were dark brown or rust colored.

Col waited till the female came quite close, and then he began to display. He bowed several times, fluffed his feathers and spread his wings, and said something that sounded like *Hwa-hwa-hwa!* He strutted around the female, too, especially when she pretended that she wanted to go away.

After a while the two bobwhites began to walk through the fencerow together. They picked up a few seeds from the ground, and the female ate several insects which Col caught for her. By that time she was ready to become his mate.

All male bobwhites choose their territory, and some of them choose the place for the nest. But Col let his mate do that. She

46

began the nest, too, by scraping a bowl-shaped hollow in the ground. Col helped her line the bowl with dead grass and small weed stems. Then he stood up in the nest and pulled grass over it, making a curved roof. It was not tight enough to keep out rain, but it would hide the nest from animals that might come near.

Soon after the nest was built, Col's mate laid a white egg in it. She laid another egg every day for two weeks, until there were fifteen eggs. As soon as the fifteenth egg was laid she began to incubate.

The eggs took more than three weeks to develop, and then all fifteen hatched in just a few hours. The young birds, or chicks, were covered with buff and brown down, and their eyes were open. As soon as their down was dry they stood up and were ready to leave the nest. Col and his mate led them through the fencerow, where they caught small insects. Their parents did not have to find food for them or put it into their mouths.

One morning, as the bobwhites were feeding, a dog came

Killdeer are shore birds that often live and build their nests on dry land. The spruce grouse (right) is a ground-dwelling bird that sometimes perches and feeds in trees.

through the field. The little birds hid and so did Col, but his mate fell down on the ground and began to flutter, as if she were badly hurt.

The mother bird was not hurt, of course. She was doing what instinct made her do when any large animal seemed to threaten her young ones. She made so much fuss that the dog saw her and followed her as she fluttered along. He did not notice that she was going farther and farther away from the chicks, and he was much surprised when she finally got up and flew to the fencerow. As soon as the dog went away, the mother bird and Col called their chicks together under a bush.

. . . . .

All kinds of quails build their nests and walk about on the ground, and so do many other birds. Still others nest and find their food on the ground, but do not stay there all the time. Some of these birds fly only short distances, but many fly as far and as well as birds that nest in trees.

The dusky grouse and spruce grouse are two birds that nest on the ground and find most of their food there. They never fly very high or very far, but sometimes they perch in low fir trees and eat the new, tender needles.

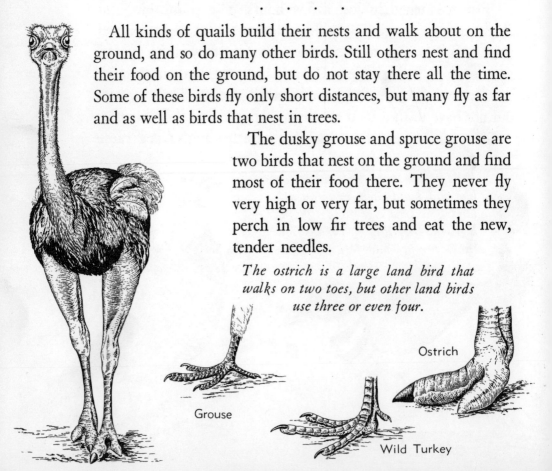

The ostrich is a large land bird that walks on two toes, but other land birds use three or even four.

Ostrich

Grouse

Wild Turkey

The killdeer is a well-known bird that nests on the ground and acts as if it were wounded when people or dogs come near its babies. Killdeer belong to the shore birds (page 54), and those that live near lakes or the sea get their food from shallow water. Killdeer also fly long distances. Many that nest in the central part of the United States go to South America for the winter and then come back again.

One good way to tell ground birds from those that perch in trees is to look at their feet. Perching birds have long, slender toes that curl tightly around branches or twigs. Three of these toes are in front, and one more is behind.

Birds that walk on the ground need feet of a different kind. Their front toes spread out flatly and rest firmly on the ground, and they generally have thick claws that can be used for scratching in the dirt. But the hind toes are not so important. Most walking birds have hind toes that are short, like Col's. Others, such as the killdeer, have no hind toes at all.

The largest ground-dwelling bird is the ostrich, which lives in Africa. Ostriches grow to be eight or nine feet tall and weigh as much as two hundred pounds. Their wings are so small that they cannot fly, and they never perch in trees. Each foot has two toes that point forward, and one toe is much larger than the other. The ostrich can walk and run very well with its two-toed feet, either on solid ground or across sandy deserts. When a large ostrich is frightened it takes twelve-foot strides and runs faster than most horses.

Young herring gulls are dark, but old ones have gray and white bodies.

Gulls, Terns, and Shore Birds

A FLOCK of herring gulls was flying above a bay. Some of the birds spread their wings and soared round and round, going so high they could hardly be seen. Others stayed close to the water. They flapped their wings when they came too near it or when they wanted to make a quick turn.

After a while the gulls flew down and began to alight on the beach. The old birds were pearl gray and white, with black on the long feathers of their wings. Young birds were brownish gray with white streaks on their necks and heads. They would take three or four years to change to the colors of their parents.

Some of the gulls stood on one leg and looked as if they were sleeping. Others walked about on the beach, making three-toed tracks. Their hind toes were so short that they did not touch the sand.

Though the gulls could walk very well, their feet were specially good for swimming. This was shown by the "webs" of pink skin that spread between the three long toes. When a gull sat on the water and spread its toes, the webs made broad paddles. The bird swam easily by moving them to and fro.

The gulls rested for a while, but soon they began to feel hungry. Some walked at the edge of the water, picking up crabs and smaller creatures that had been washed ashore. One gull found a clam, but its shell was so thick that he could not break it with his beak. He picked the clam up, took it high into the air, and dropped it on a paved highway that ran along the shore. When the shell broke the gull swooped down and carried it back to the beach. There he ate the clam's soft flesh, but left the broken shell on the sand.

While this herring gull was eating his clam some of his neighbors went fishing. They flew close to the water and looked into it. When one of the gulls saw a fish he darted down and caught it with his beak. If the fish was near the surface the gull did this so quickly that only his head and feet got wet. Other gulls picked up dead fish or bits of garbage that had been thrown from ships.

· · · ·

There are many kinds of gulls in many different parts of the world. They also live in many different places. Some make their homes on rocky coasts where waves splash every day. Other gulls like low, sandy shores or lakes, rivers and swamps that are hundreds of miles from the sea. Many build their nests on steep cliffs, but others prefer stony beaches, grassy islands, or the

Franklin's gulls live far from the sea. They often eat grubs and insects in fields.

ground in open woods. Herring gulls whose eggs are often stolen by people learn to put their nests in trees that are too tall for nest-robbers to climb.

As soon as the young birds can take care of themselves, many gulls leave the places where they nest. Some go to seashores or lakes farther south, but others go to the harbors of cities such as New York, San Francisco, and New Orleans. These harbor gulls perch on buildings, posts, and ships, or walk about on docks. When night comes they often fly down to the water and float there while they sleep.

Gulls can live in different habitats because they do not need special surroundings or eat special kinds of food. Herring gulls seem to like lakes and rivers as well as seashores, and the California gull nests on islands in lakes surrounded by deserts or among mountains that are covered with forests. Laughing gulls lay their eggs on sandy beaches, among tall grass, or under bushes and vines.

Fish is the favorite food of most gulls, but crabs and other creatures seem to please the birds almost as well. Gulls that stay near harbors often feed at garbage dumps or eat the waste and scraps that are thrown from places where fish are canned or dried. Gulls whose homes are beside lakes or swamps often go to newly-plowed fields to pick up grubs and beetles. They also catch great numbers of grasshoppers and other harmful insects. Flocks of Franklin's gulls once helped the pioneer farmers in Utah, for the birds ate millions of big grasshoppers (called Mormon crickets) which were destroying the farmers' crops.

. . . .

Terns are web-footed birds that are smaller and more slender than gulls. You can tell them by their long wings, forked tails, and sharp beaks. Most terns are white and pale gray, with black on their heads, but one kind is dark gray and black during the spring and summer.

Common terns are smaller than gulls and have forked tails. They fly swiftly and often dive for food.

Sanderlings are small shore birds that can walk, wade or swim.

Terns eat almost nothing except fish, so they never go very far from water. They fly with their heads and beaks turned downward. When a tern sees a fish he dives to catch it. The hungry bird does not mind going completely under water.

Gulls and terns nest on shores and are sometimes called shore birds, but another group really deserves this name. Most of these birds both nest on the shore and get their food there, eating snails, crabs and insects which they find in mud or wet sand. These shore birds have long beaks, long legs, and wings that are V-shaped when they fly. A few have small webs between their toes, but none of them swims as much as gulls and terns do.

Sandpipers are common shore birds, and sanderlings are common sandpipers. They are little grayish brown and white birds that scrape out saucer-shaped nests in the sand and line them with grass or leaves. The babies run about soon after they hatch, just as young bobwhites do.

When fall comes, sanderlings begin to live in little flocks. They rest, run, and fly together, and each bird can twist or turn in the air at the same time as his neighbors. When sanderlings are hungry they run along the shore, looking for things to eat. They scamper away as waves come in, but turn and follow the water as it goes back to the sea. Sometimes the birds go into the water so far that their legs are covered, but they do not dive.

We say that *most* shore birds get their food from muddy or sandy shores because some kinds, or species, often live far from water. The killdeer, for example, may nest far from shores and feed on land-dwelling insects. Wilson's snipes live on meadows and in marshes, where they hide in tall grass. Woodcocks like marshes, too, but they often make their homes in woods or on hills. There the birds catch grasshoppers or other insects and pull earthworms out of the ground.

One more surprising fact is this: Many shore birds that have no webs on their toes can swim as well as those that have them. Sanderlings, for example, often fly long distances over the ocean. When they grow tired they come down and rest on the water, where they swim as easily as gulls.

Tattler, a yellowlegs, hunting food near the shore of a lake.

Birds That Wade in Shallow Water

TATTLER, a yellowlegs, was hunting his breakfast near the shore of a lake. He walked to and fro in the shallow water, watching for small fish and insects. When he saw one he caught it with his long beak and swallowed it in just one gulp.

Tattler could swim when he wanted to, but wading was better for hunting. He sometimes hurried through water that just covered his toes, but he moved slowly when the water came up to his knees. A bird's knees, of course, are close to its body and are hidden by feathers. When Tattler waded in water that came to his knees, he looked as if he were swimming slowly and jerkily.

As soon as the yellowlegs finished his breakfast, he flew over the lake. He went round and round in big circles, calling *Wheu-wheu-wheu!* Then he came back to the muddy shore close to the place where he had been feeding. When he alighted he raised his long wings over his back and held them there for an instant. As he did so, his tail and the lower part of his back shone white. But when he folded his wings the clear white disappeared under feathers so finely streaked with black and white that they seemed to be gray.

Tattler stood quietly after he folded his wings, looking up and down the shore. Then he tucked one long yellow leg under his feathers. He balanced himself on the other leg and closed his eyes to rest.

The yellowlegs seemed to be asleep, but he really was wide awake. He listened to everything that went on near his part of the lake shore. He heard geese call as they flew overhead, and listened to ducks that paddled about in the shallow water. He also heard a flock of small sandpipers twitter as they ran along the shore. Their wings went *Whir-rr, whir-rr!* when they flew toward him.

Tattler knew all these sounds, and they did not alarm him. But when he heard a man's steps he called *Klar, Klaar!* loudly and flew away as fast as he could.

The ducks and sandpipers flew away too, for they knew that Tattler's calls meant "Danger!" The ducks went to the other side of the lake and hid among tall grass and cat-tails. The sandpipers did not go so far. They flew over the water in a long curve that finally brought them back to the shore. There they landed on a gravelly bank where they could hardly be seen.

Tattler did not come back to the lake shore, as the small sandpipers did. He flew higher and higher into the air and then started toward the ocean. It was so far away that he could not see it, but he seemed to know just where it was.

The yellowlegs could fly rapidly, for his wings were long and strong. He flew above farms, woodlands and towns until he saw the ocean. Then he turned and traveled southward along the white line made by waves that splashed on the rocky coast.

Tattler flew on and on until he saw that the coast became sandy, and the sand was piled into hills known as dunes. Behind the dunes were ponds and marshes where tall, coarse grass grew in salt water. Tattler flew down to the shore of a pond where a dozen other yellowlegs were resting or catching fish. Some of them called *Wheu-wheu-wheu!* as if they were saying "Hello" or "Stop and rest!"

Tattler was glad to have company, but he was not tired enough to rest. He folded his wings and walked into the water, where he caught some small fish for his supper. When evening came he flew to a sandbar and went to sleep.

Sandhill cranes often wade in swamps. They fly with their necks stretched out.

Tattler shows us that birds which are closely related may not have quite the same habits. Yellowlegs are true shore birds that belong in the same family with sandpipers, woodcocks, and snipes. Yet yellowlegs do not run along beaches like sandpipers, or dig in mud for their food, as snipes do. Yellowlegs also never live on land among thick forests, where woodcocks often make their homes.

The families to which birds belong may not tell us much about their habits, and habits may tell nothing at all about families and other relationships. Wading birds, for example, belong to three different groups that are not closely related. One group, as we know, contains Tattler and his relatives, which are only big, long-legged sandpipers. Others have special names, such as willet, godwit, and stilt.

Cranes are a small group of wading birds that may also live on dry, grassy land. The largest members of this group are whooping cranes, which are big white birds with very loud

A Louisiana heron and a flamingo (right).
The heron crooks its neck when it flies.

voices. They nest far away in the North, and have been hunted so much that they are very rare.

Sandhill cranes are gray instead of white, and they are not so rare. They often wade in grassy swamps and build their nests in the water, but they also live on prairies where they hunt mice, insects, and snakes instead of fish and frogs. When cranes fly they stretch their necks and hold their legs straight behind them.

Herons belong to the largest group of wading birds. It is so big that scientists divide it into smaller groups, such as storks, ibises, and flamingos.

Herons are somtimes called "cranes," but that is a mistake. We can tell herons by their sharp beaks and their necks, which are S-shaped when the birds fly. Herons also nest in trees, not on the ground, where cranes build their nests.

Great blue herons wade into the water and stand still till fish or frogs come near them. But Louisiana herons walk about, just

Wood ibises hunt food in grassy swamps but build their nests in trees. These birds are the only American storks.

as yellowlegs do. Sometimes they even chase fish or tadpoles that swim into very shallow water and then try to get away. Louisiana herons are bluish gray, white and brown, and are common birds in swamps of the southern United States.

The wood ibis is another southern bird, but it likes grassy swamps better than those that are full of trees. The wood ibis really is a stork—the only stork that lives in North America. It is a large white bird with black on its tail and wings. Its head and neck are bare and dark, and its beak curves downward. When it flies it holds its neck out straight, like a sandhill crane. But it builds its nest in a tree, just as if it were a heron.

Flamingos are rose-pink wading birds which we sometimes see in parks and zoos. They have long, thin necks and very long legs, and their short, thick beaks are bent downward. They scoop up mud and strain out small animals and plants with the sievelike sides of their beaks.

. . . .

Though some wading birds live on dry land, most of them make their homes in shallow-water habitats. Some, such as cranes, may nest in the water, but most of them like the ground or trees that grow in swampy places.

Immer, a loon, and his mate playing on a lake.

Immer and Other Divers

IMMER, a loon, gave a call that sounded like *Who-who-who,* said several times in a voice that was loud and high. The call wakened Immer's mate, who began to swim beside him. They went round and round in big circles. Then they stood up above the surface of their lake and flapped their wings several times.

After Immer flapped his wings he went fishing. He swam low down, like a submarine that had not quite "surfaced." Now and then he put his head under water, keeping his eyes open so he could look for fish. When he saw one he dived swiftly, caught it, and came back to the surface. There he shook the fish, swallowed it, and began to look for food again.

Immer could swim very well, for his body was streamlined and his webbed feet made fine, strong paddles. He could skim along at the surface and could even walk on the water by moving his feet rapidly and flapping his black-and-white wings. He also could sink just as much as he wanted to. Sometimes he swam with his whole body under water. Only his black head could be seen at the surface.

People often call loons "great northern divers," since they nest in the North and are larger than other diving birds. They are swifter than most other divers, too, for they can use their wings as oars. In this way they can swim under water much faster than birds that use only their feet.

Although loons are swift and graceful in the water, they are slow and awkward on land. Immer and his mate waddled clumsily when they went to their nest on the shore. Their legs were so near their tails that both loons flapped their wings to keep from falling. When Immer tripped on a branch, he did tumble over with a thump.

Neither Immer nor his mate ever tried to fly from the land. Both birds always "took off" from the water. There they could run along the surface, paddling on it with their webbed feet while their wings beat faster and faster. At last they rose into the air, where they used their feet as rudders to steer to the right or left. They could not turn quickly, as gulls and sanderlings do.

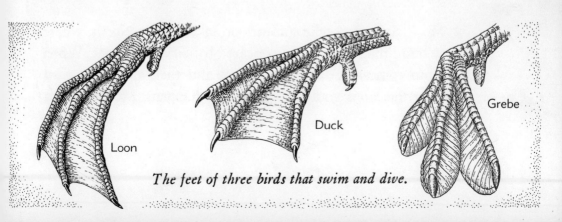

Loon   Duck   Grebe

The feet of three birds that swim and dive.

After flying as long as they wanted to, the loons always came down, or "landed," on water. They struck it with a loud splash and then skittered to a stop. This means that they flew along just above the surface, touching it several times while their wings beat more and more slowly. At last they stopped flying and began to swim.

· · · ·

One day, as the loons called and flapped their wings, they frightened two grebes that were feeding in the lake. They bent their necks and dived almost as well as Immer could do.

Although grebes dive and sometimes eat fish, they are not exactly like loons. No grebe becomes as big as Immer or has such a thick, strong beak. Loons' feet have webs that connect their three front toes, but a grebe's toes are not connected. Each has its separate web, which spreads out like flaps on both sides of the toe.

Grebes are almost as awkward as loons on land, but they seldom go there. For grebes, as we know, build their nests in the water. Some nests are piled up into little islands, but others float and are fastened to cat-tails or reeds. The old birds swim to these nests and swim away when they leave them. That's much easier than waddling, flapping their wings, and tripping or tumbling, as loons do when they go ashore.

· · · ·

Most loons spend the summer on lakes in the North, where they build their nests and take care of their young ones. When autumn comes the lakes grow cold and then are covered by ice, but the loons go away before that happens. Most of them

64

travel southward and to seashores, where the salty water does not freeze.

Loons that spend the winter along the seacoast see many other birds that swim, eat fish, and dive. One of these is the cormorant, or "shag." It is a big, black bird with a slender neck and a hook at the end of its beak. It can dive and catch fish as well as a loon. Cormorants like to rest on rocks beside the water, half-spreading their wings in the sunshine. You can easily tell a cormorant by its half-spread wings.

Water turkeys, or *anhingas* (an hing′ gaz), look rather like cormorants with straight beaks. They live among swamps or on seashores, but never come north to the places where loons spend the winter. Water turkeys can dive by sinking into the water from the surface, but they also plunge into it from trees where they rest and build their nests.

The anhinga, or water turkey, often dives from the trees in which it perches and nests.

The dark ducks called surf scoters often dive into shallow water for clams and scallops, not fish. Scoters also go on shore when the tide is low, to eat the purplish black mussels that live among rocks and on mud. The ducks swallow pebbles while they are eating and use them to grind their food.

The little dovekie is a diving bird only eight inches long. In the summer it nests in holes among loose rocks on cliffs, far away in the North. Each mother bird lays only one egg, and the nestling is fed on tiny shrimplike creatures. But as soon as the young ones are able to fly, dovekies go out to the ocean. There they live in huge flocks, swimming in the cold water and diving for small fish. In the winter they go southward along the coasts of North America and Europe. Loons often see them during the coldest months, but when March and April come the dovekies go northward again.

The penguin is another kind of diving bird, but it never visits places where loons spend the winter. Penguins live in the southern half of the earth, and we can see them only in zoos. Their feet are so near their tails that they can stand and walk upright, like people. When they swim or dive they use their wings, which make fine oars but are much too small to be used in flying.

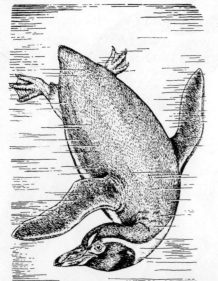

Penguins use their wings when they swim under water. These birds live south of the Equator, and even in Antarctica.

Birds with Different Habitats

SPONSA, a mother wood duck, spent a whole day trying to find a place for her nest. She did not look on the ground, for wood ducks nest in trees. They like hollow trunks or branches, but sometimes they use holes that were dug by woodpeckers.

Father Wood Duck went with his mate, but he did not choose the nesting place. First he sat on a dead branch while she poked her head into a hole that seemed too small. Then he followed Sponsa from one tree to another in the woods around a swampy pond. But not one of those trees contained a large hole, so the mother wood duck led her mate farther and farther into the woods.

At last Sponsa spied a big, old oak tree that stood near the middle of the woods. Part of the trunk was dead and had decayed, and there Sponsa found a hole about twenty feet above the ground. She slipped into the hole, sat down in it, and turned round two or three times. When she came out she did not look for any more holes. This one was just what she wanted, even though it was far away from the pond.

A gray squirrel had once lived in the oak tree and had made a bed of dead leaves in the hole. Sponsa covered the leaves with soft downy feathers which she pulled from her breast. The down and the dead leaves made a very good nest. While Sponsa lined her nest, Father Wood Duck sat on a branch and preened himself. He acted as if he was proud of his spring, or nuptial (nup′ shal), colors, which were brighter than those of other ducks. His feathers were green, brown, purple, and dark yellow, and they had black and white markings. The silky feathers that covered his head and hung down behind it gleamed when the sun shone on them.

For two weeks the wood ducks stayed at the pond, where they ate insects, tadpoles, and minnows. But Sponsa flew to her nest-hole every day, and on every day except one she laid a cream-colored egg. At last, when the nest contained thirteen eggs, she began to incubate, or sit.

Many male birds take turns sitting on the eggs, but Father Wood Duck did not. He did stay near the nest for several days, but then he spent more and more time at the pond. He also began to change his feathers, or *molt*. His bright-colored nuptial feathers fell out one by one, and new feathers grew in their place. These new feathers made him look almost the same as Sponsa.

Father Wood Duck could not fly when his long wing feathers fell out. He had to stay on the pond all

Father Wood Duck waited while his mate looked for a nesting hole.

Sponsa flew from her hole in the tree to the ground.

the time, hiding among cat-tails and long grass until his new feathers were long enough to be used.

Sponsa's eggs began to hatch just twenty-nine days after she had laid the last one. The babies were not bare-skinned and helpless, like the young of most birds that nest in trees. The little wood ducks were covered with fluffy down, like newly hatched bobwhites and killdeer. Their dark eyes were open, too, and they soon began to move about as if they wanted to leave the nest.

Some wood duck babies leave the nest a few hours after they hatch and flutter down to the ground or to a pond. Sponsa's little ones stayed in the hollow tree for a day. Then their mother flew to the ground and called softly till the babies climbed out of the nest. Soon they jumped, beat their tiny wings, and fluttered down beside their mother. Their coats of down kept them from falling too fast, though they were not strong enough to fly.

When all the nestlings were on the ground, Sponsa said *Chip-cheep, chee-eep!* This seemed to mean "Follow me, children," for when Sponsa started toward the pond the little ones walked behind her. When she came to the water and started to swim, the little ones did so too. Next day they were able to catch small insects and nip soft leaves. Sponsa found things to eat and kept watch for danger, but she did not give food to her babies.

. . . . .

Different kinds of birds differ in their choice of habitats. Some live only in one kind of place, and so are marsh birds, woodland birds, or sea birds. Others, like loons, live in one habitat during the summer but go to a different one in the winter. Still other kinds can live in several habitats, or can change from one habitat to another. If they were people we might say that they are "easily pleased."

A better word for these birds is "adaptable." It means that they can build their nests, find food, and live in different habi-

Say's phoebe lives on low, hot deserts as well as in the cool North.

Mockingbirds live in deserts, where the weather is hot and dry, as well as in parts of the country that are moist and have many trees.

tats as well as under different conditions. The robin is an adaptable bird, for it makes its home in woods or orchards, near farm buildings or in cities, and among mountains, on prairies, or along seacoasts. It eats berries, insects, earthworms, and small animals that hide among pebbles on the shore.

Blue jays are adaptable and so are mockingbirds, which live among moist green woods in the Southeast and on dry southwestern deserts. Say's phoebe (fee´ bie) is a very adaptable western bird, for it nests in caves and on cliffs, in barns and empty houses, under bridges, and even in wells. It also is found in many different regions, from cool, moist valleys of Alaska to the lowest, hottest, driest deserts in the Southwest.

Adaptable birds often are more abundant than birds that can live in only one habitat. You already know that robins and blue jays are common. Can you name a few other common birds that live in several habitats?

71

Male and female house sparrows, which are also called English sparrows.

Large and Small Ranges

CHIRP, a house sparrow, was hopping along a sidewalk. He bounced along on both feet. He could not walk by moving one foot at a time, as bobwhites and many other birds do.

As Chirp hopped he kept watch for food. Children who went along the sidewalk often dropped bits of popcorn or cookies. Chirp soon found a cookie which some child had lost.

Other sparrows that saw Chirp pick up the cookie began to fly or hop toward him. Some were dull brownish gray birds, but others had black throats, dull white cheeks, and reddish brown on the sides of their heads. The dull birds were females, but those with brighter colors were males. Chirp was a male sparrow, for he had a black throat and white cheeks.

As soon as these other sparrows came close, they tried to get Chirp's cookie. They chattered and pushed and pecked until they broke the cookie to pieces. Chirp took one piece and flew away to the top of an electric sign. Even there he had to fight to keep other sparrows from taking his food.

When the cookie was eaten, the other sparrows paid no more attention to Chirp. He hopped along the sidewalk again, dodging when people walked toward him. Then he flew to a tall apartment house, where a woman often put crumbs on her window sill. Chirp ate the largest crumbs. Then he sat in the sun for a while, watching automobiles go past on the street.

House sparrows have big appetites, but they get food in many places. They find cookies and other things on sidewalks, and they pick up scraps that fall from trucks that haul garbage away from restaurants. Sparrows also hunt insects in city parks, find crumbs beside benches where people lunch, and eat other

Ranges of the house sparrow and bald eagle in North America. The sparrow is common in all parts of its range, but the bald eagle generally is rare.

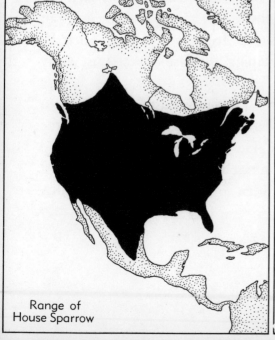

Range of
House Sparrow

Range of
Bald Eagle

Kirtland's warbler has a very small nesting range in northern Michigan. It is shown in black on the map.

crumbs which people put on window sills. City birds also find weed seeds in vacant lots. Country sparrows get much of their food in barnyards and chicken pens.

Though Chirp was busy from morning till night, he took a dust bath every dry, warm day. He liked to squat down in the dry dirt of a garden, a flower bed, or even a window box. He shook his feathers till the dust sifted through them and out again, taking away loose bits of feathers and dirt. Then he preened himself carefully, wiping the last bits of dust away with his beak.

On rainy days Chirp changed from his dust bath to one in a puddle of water. He always chose very shallow pools, where the water just covered his toes. He fluffed out his feathers and splashed, and then preened himself just as he did after a dust bath. Of course, he used his beak to wipe away water, not tiny bits of dust.

74

We soon decide that house sparrows are very adaptable birds. They can eat many kinds of food, which they find in many different places. They also can live on farms, in towns, or in big cities, and they nest in trees or on buildings. They seem to like warm climates almost as well as cold ones, and they appear to be happy where rain and snow often fall, as well as where the weather is dry during most of the year.

This explains why house sparrows are common, and it helps explain why they have a large *range*. This means that they live in many places, in many parts of the world. There are house sparrows in Europe, Asia, and North America. The birds live in Australia and New Zealand, too, and on many small islands.

House sparrows have been in some of these places so long that we do not know how they got there. But people took them from Europe to North America, to Australia, and to New Zealand. House sparrows were brought from England to North America in 1850. That is why we often call these birds English sparrows.

A California condor and its young. These birds have a very small range.

Most adaptable birds have large ranges, but birds that are not adaptable have small ones. The Kirtland's warbler has a very small summer range, for it is found in just a few counties in northern Michigan. There it nests on the sandy ground under young jack pines and scrub oaks that grow after forest fires. The warbler will not go anywhere else, and it will not nest in places where the pine trees and oaks become more than twelve to eighteen feet high.

The California condor also is not adaptable, and it has such a small range that it may soon die out. This condor is a big black and white bird that really is a kind of vulture. Condors once were killed by hunters and by poisoned meat which ranchmen put out for wolves. Killing is now forbidden by law, but the birds are not becoming common. Though no one knows just why, scientists think it is because condors do not like human beings. The birds may not nest or have young ones when people are near. Since there are not many parts of our country where condors can stay far away from people, the birds now have a very small range in California and northern Mexico. Even there condors live only among steep mountains where almost no one goes.

Bird Travels, or Migrations

HONKER, a young wild goose, was feeding in a swamp. First she nipped tender leaves from plants that grew above the surface. Then she reached into the water and pulled up some thick white roots. She also ate some snails which she found on the muddy bottom.

Honker was a wild bird, but many kinds of geese are wild. She belonged to the kind called the Canada goose, although it often lives in the United States. Some Canada geese nest as far south as the states of Tennessee and Arizona.

Honker did not know her name, of course, and she did not know about Canada geese that nested in the South. She had hatched beside a lake in the North, not far from Hudson Bay. There she stayed all summer with her parents and her five brothers and sisters. But when autumn came they joined a flock that went to the swamp to feed. They ate so much that they soon became fat and strong. They were ready to fly to their winter home, which was two thousand miles away.

An old male goose, or gander, gave the signal to start on a frosty morning in October. When he called, the whole flock flapped into the air and flew in a big circle. But soon the old gander went ahead, and the other geese formed two lines behind him. Both lines spread out and formed a big V.

Canada geese are not the only birds that fly in a V behind their leader. Other geese, some ducks, and herring gulls do so. Each bird in the flock flies close to the one in front of him, but a little way to one side. This lets every bird look ahead and gives him room to beat his wings. Each beat also makes little whirlpools of air. The whirl made by the *outside* wing tip of one bird helps to lift the *inside* wing tip of the bird just behind. This makes flying easier for all birds except the leader. Since he is at the front of the V, he has to fly without any help.

The geese flew on and on at a rate of forty to fifty miles per hour. But at noon the leader guided them to a marshy lake. As the geese came down they held their wings stiffly and glided

Canada geese generally fly in V's when they travel, or migrate. Here a flock is coming down to swim and feed in a swampy lake.

to the surface. None of them splashed into the water as Immer, the loon, always did.

The geese found many other birds resting and feeding at the lake. There were two or three kinds of ducks, and grebes that dived into the water for minnows, worms, and insects. A couple of loons were diving, too, but they caught larger fish and frogs.

The geese swam about and preened their feathers until they were ready to eat. Some ate leaves and roots in the lake, but many went to a meadow where they picked up seeds and caught insects. The old birds kept watch while the others fed. The guards stood on the highest places they could find, holding their necks up straight as they looked and listened for danger.

The geese stayed at the swampy lake for two days and then traveled southward again. Sometimes they flew from morning till late afternoon, and sometimes they stopped to feed after flying two or three hours. Now and then they flew at night but rested and fed during the daytime.

One night a bad storm came up while the geese were flying. Rain pelted down, the wind blew hard, and the sky became so dark that the geese could not see their neighbors. The two lines of the V stretched out and became irregular, but the birds called, or honked, so often that no one strayed away. Honker followed the calls easily, until the leader guided the flock to a lake that made a good stopping place.

When a flock of geese flies more than two or three hours, it always changes leaders. As the first leader grows tired he drops back into one of the lines and another bird takes his place. The new leader is always a strong old gander that has made the trip before. He knows where to go and where to stop, so the flock can rest safely and find plenty of food.

Big flocks, in which there are hundreds of geese, often divide when they fly. Each part of the flock may form a V, or there may be three or four V's and a couple of slanting lines. Honker's flock was not big enough for that, but it sometimes got into trouble while the leaders were changing. When that happened the geese flew close together or in zigzags. But as soon as the new leader got his place, the lines straightened out and formed a V again.

. . . .

As the geese flew or stopped to feed, they met many other birds that also were traveling. They came from many different places, but all were going toward the South.

These bird travelers were *migrating,* or going from one place to another at a regular time in the year. Most birds that nest in the North migrate southward to their winter homes and come northward again in the spring. But some kinds do not follow this rule. Birds that live among mountains often go into valleys for the winter instead of flying away to the South. Many herons and eagles travel northward after their nesting season and then go southward again in the fall.

The part of the country in which a kind of bird nests and brings up its young ones is its *summer,* or *breeding, range.* The region where it spends the winter is its *winter range.* Canada geese have a very large breeding range—all the way from Arizona and Tennessee to northern Canada. Their winter range is large too, for they may stay almost anywhere in the United States.

You might think some Canada geese would not migrate, but that would be a mistake. Geese that nest in the United States migrate southward in the fall, going to California, Florida, or swamps near the Gulf of Mexico. Geese that nest in Canada fly to the United States. Honker's flock, which came from northern Canada, spent the winter on Delaware Bay, less than a hundred miles south of New York City.

Some birds, such as house sparrows, cardinals, and screech owls, do not migrate and some others migrate only once in a while. Snowy owls (page 83), for example, generally stay in the North, but when food becomes scarce they travel southward.

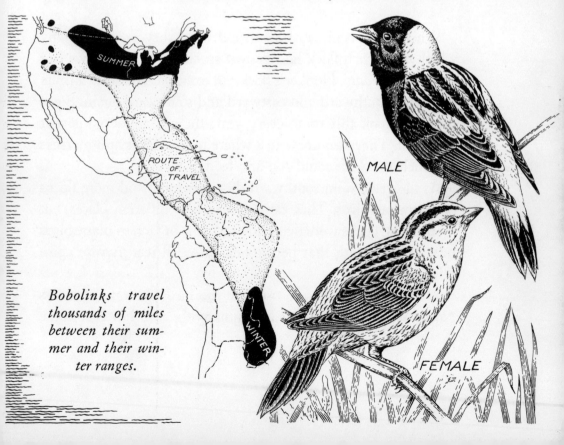

SUMMER

ROUTE
OF
TRAVEL

WINTER

Bobolinks travel thousands of miles between their summer and their winter ranges.

MALE

FEMALE

Then people see them sitting on fence posts or chimneys in the central part of the United States as well as in southern Canada.

Some chickadees and bluebirds migrate, but others do not. The eastern bluebird has a breeding range that extends from Florida and Texas to southern Canada. Bluebirds that nest in the South stay near their homes in the winter, but those that nest in the North migrate. By December, almost all eastern bluebirds are south of Missouri and New York.

Other birds travel long distances between their breeding ranges and winter ranges. One long-distance traveler is the bobolink, which goes from the northern part of the United States and southern Canada to South America. This means a round trip of six to eight thousand miles!

. . . .

When birds begin to travel southward they do not go any which-way. Each flock has its own special path, which we call a *migration route*. Honker's flock, for example, followed a route that went southward and eastward and southward again. Since the geese took this route every year, the old ganders knew it very well. They also knew just where to find lakes and marshes in which the flock could rest and feed.

As the geese went southward they met more and more flocks of migrating birds. They came from many different places, but soon all the flocks were flying in one path. In fact, so many birds followed this path that people began to call it a *flyway,* not a migration route.

Four great flyways are used by the birds that travel across North America. One flyway begins with branches that come

82

from the North. After the branches join, this flyway follows the Atlantic coast to Florida and then to South America.

Another flyway also begins with branches from the North, but it goes down the valleys of the Missouri and Mississippi Rivers. Many birds that use this flyway then go east or west to spend the winter near the Gulf of Mexico.

The two other flyways are in the West. One comes southward east of the Rocky Mountains and the other is near the Pacific coast. But in some places these flyways spread out, divide and overlap. A flock of birds in Utah, for example, may be traveling in either the Central or the Pacific Flyway.

When spring comes, birds that have traveled southward go back to their summer homes. Most of them fly along the same flyways and routes which they took in the fall. Flocks may even stop to rest and feed in the very same places!

Snowy owls migrate south-ward in winter, but only when food becomes scarce in the North.

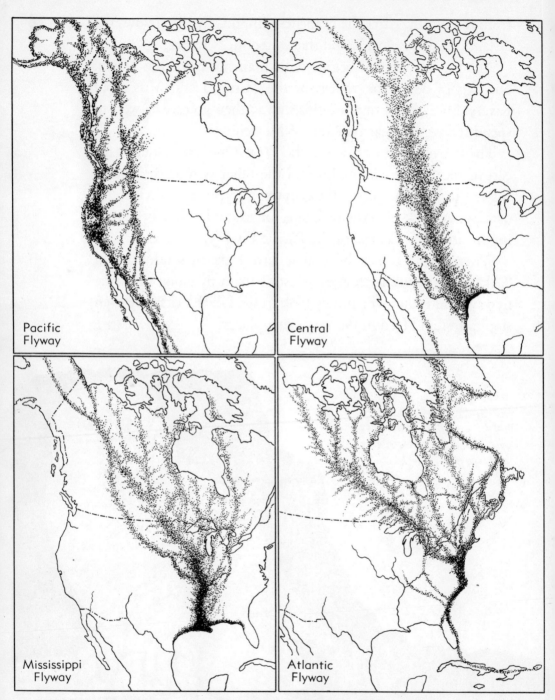

Pacific
Flyway

Central
Flyway

Mississippi
Flyway

Atlantic
Flyway

*The four great routes, or flyways, which North American
birds use when they travel.*

Feathers and Colors

BRIGHT, a rose-breasted grosbeak, began to migrate southward late in September, just as autumn was beginning. Since he lived in Illinois he traveled along the Mississippi Flyway. If he had been an eastern bird, he would have gone along the western edge of the Atlantic Flyway.

Though Bright was a rose-breasted grosbeak, most of his feathers were not red. He had black-and-white wings and a black tail, and his back was light and dark brown. There were black spots on his sides, and only his breast was rose-pink. He seemed to disappear when he perched in bushes, for his colors made him look like shadows, dead leaves, and twigs.

Bright traveled with a flock of about thirty other grosbeaks. Some were old males, like Bright. Others were females, with brown instead of black on their wings and tails, and no pink on their breasts. Young males also were brown, buff and white, but they had pink feathers on their breasts.

The grosbeaks did not hurry as they migrated southward. Every night they flew for several hours, but then they stopped to rest in woodlands, in bushy places, or even in city parks. When morning came they began to feed. They ate seeds from bushes and weeds of various kinds, but they also caught many insects. They were specially fond of small beetles. The birds cracked beetle shells between their thick beaks, just as if the insects were seeds.

Though the grosbeaks did not fly very far at one time, they kept on going night after night. They soon passed the city of St. Louis, where electric lights made the sky look hazy yellow at night. The flock passed Memphis, Vicksburg, and New Orleans, too, and crossed the Gulf of Mexico. There the birds flew 350 miles without stopping. They did this because there was no land between the United States and Mexico, and because perching birds such as grosbeaks do not like to rest on the sea.

As Bright and his friends traveled southward, they met more and more flocks of rose-breasted grosbeaks. They came from all parts of the birds' breeding range. As you can see from the map, this extends from the Atlantic Ocean to the Rocky Mountains, and from the mountains of Georgia to northern Canada.

A male rose-breasted grosbeak in the fall. The map shows how these birds travel from their summer to their winter homes.

The map also shows that rose-breasted grosbeaks follow a route that grows narrower and narrower after it reaches Mexico. Some of the birds stay there all winter, but others go to different parts of Central America or cross the Isthmus of Panama. Then the route spreads out again as flocks go to their winter homes in South America. Bright and his friends went to a forest in the country called Ecuador (Ek′ wa dore).

The weather in Ecuador was warm, and the grosbeaks found plenty of insects and many kinds of seeds. They also saw great numbers of birds. Some never left South America, but others had come from Canada and the United States.

As the warm southern winter came to an end, the grosbeaks began to molt. Some of them also changed their colors, but many others did not.

The birds that did not change were females, and their molt was very incomplete. This means that they lost only a few old feathers and grew only a few new ones. The new feathers also had just the same colors as those that had fallen out.

Young males also had an incomplete molt, but they made some changes. Their breasts became pale red and new black feathers grew on their tails. Though they kept most of the old brown feathers in their wings, some new ones became black and white.

A male rose-breasted grosbeak in the spring.

Old males, such as Bright, changed most of all. Bright kept last-year's feathers on his wings and tail but got new ones on his head and body. His new feathers were black and white, except for a deep rose-red patch on his breast. Bright was very handsome after his spring molt.

When the time came to migrate northward, the male grosbeaks started first. They took the same narrow route across the Isthmus of Panama and Central America, and they met more and more flocks of grosbeaks as they came to Mexico. After that the flocks began to separate as they went to different parts of their nesting range. Bright's flock flew straight to the Mississippi Flyway and followed it to their summer home in Illinois.

. . . .

Birds have many different colors and use them in different ways. The dull colors which all rose-breasted grosbeaks wear in the fall keep the birds from being seen while they rest and hunt food. But the black, white and red which old males put on in the spring can be seen very easily. They seem to warn other birds to stay away after the grosbeaks choose their territories. The bright colors are like warning signs that say *"Stop!"* or *"Keep Out!"*

Perhaps the male birds' bright colors and loud songs also mean *"Welcome"* to female grosbeaks when they come from the South. A female soon saw Bright as he perched on a tree near one side of his territory. When she became his mate she built her nest in a bush that grew near the tree.

Since the female grosbeak's colors were dull, she seemed to

be part of the leaves and twigs in the bush. Hawks and squirrels did not see her as she sat on the nest. They also did not notice her when she came with food for her nestlings.

Some birds molt only once a year, but rose-breasted grosbeaks molt twice. The second time comes late in the summer, after the nesting season. In this molt the birds lose all their feathers, a few at a time, and grow new ones. The females do not change color, but old males become dull again. They can easily hide when they rest and hunt insects on their migration southward.

. . . .

Several bright-colored birds do not become dull after the nesting season. One of these is the male cardinal, which is just as red in the winter as he is in spring. Blue jays also do not change color, though they are blue, black, and white instead of red. Both cardinals and jays are strong, active birds that do not often need to hide. Jays are never afraid to quarrel with squirrels, crows, or hawks.

Some birds that do not change colors are dull instead of bright. They look so much like the ground or dead leaves or grass that we say they are camouflaged. Camouflage (kam′ uh flazh) is a French word that means hiding by looking like something else, such as the ground or dead leaves.

A bobwhite is camouflaged, for its

The cardinal does not change color or migrate after the nesting season.

feathers resemble stones and dead leaves on the ground where it lives. The American bittern looks like dry marsh grass, especially when it stands still with its beak pointed upward. Young night herons, which are grayish brown and white with buff and black streaks, also look like dry reeds and cat-tails.

Nighthawks (which are not hawks, but are relatives of the whippoorwill) are easy to see when they are flying. They also are easy to hear, for they say *Bee-eerd! Bee-eerd!* loudly. But when nighthawks rest on the ground or sit on their eggs, they are very well camouflaged. Their blackish feathers, with buff, gray and white markings, look like pebbles on the ground.

Many shore birds, such as sandpipers, are light underneath but have mixtures of dark colors on their backs. Their light breasts make them hard to see from the water or the ground. But creatures that look down upon them see their mottled backs, which seem to be part of the beaches where the shore birds feed.

Killdeer have black and white stripes across their bodies, with brown on their heads and backs. These colors seem to cut the birds up into small pieces when we see them from far away.

A nighthawk shows plainly while it is flying, but it looks like pebbles or dead leaves when it sits on the ground.

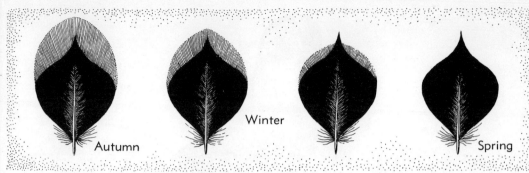

How a snow bunting's feather grows dark as it is worn down.

You will find it very hard to put all the pieces together and make them look like a bird.

Even bright colors may be hard to see. Male goldfinches are yellow with black wings in the summer, but these birds do not show plainly when they feed among yellow dandelion flowers.

Robins molt only once a year, near the end of August. Still, they seem to get bright new feathers in the spring. Starlings also molt in the summer, but they turn dark and glossy when winter comes to an end.

These changes come because the tips of feathers wear off. When robins molt the new feathers on their breasts have gray tips. During the winter those gray tips wear off. By spring robins have "new" red breasts which really are old.

The same kind of color change is made by snow buntings and starlings. When snow buntings molt, late in the summer, new feathers on their bodies and heads have dull brownish tips. As the tips wear off the buntings become black and white. Starlings also have dull, spotted tips on their feathers after they molt, but they become black, purple, and green as the dull tips wear off. The only part of a starling that really changes color in the spring is his beak. It turns from brown to yellow.

91

Crown, a kingbird, perched on a tree and watched for insects.

Protection and Defense

CROWN, an eastern kingbird, perched at the top of a tree. He turned his head from side to side, watching for insects that flew past. When he saw one he darted out to catch it, turned, and went back to his perch.

The way Crown captured insects showed that he was one of the birds which we call flycatchers. Most flycatchers are dull green or brownish gray, but eastern kingbirds are slaty gray, black and white. When they spread the black feathers on their heads, they show orange-red crowns.

Crown caught robber flies, wasps, and other insects by darting from his perch. Sometimes he also went down to the ground. There he picked up beetles, ants, crickets, and caterpillars.

The kingbird ate some of these insects, for he worked hard to catch them and needed plenty of food. But he took many more insects home to his young ones, which lived in a nest near the top of an apple tree. Crown's mate brought food to the nestlings, too. Since she looked exactly like Crown, people who saw the kingbirds sometimes thought that he did all the work.

When the kingbirds took food to their young ones, they did not go straight to the nest. Instead, they flew close to the ground and slipped quietly through some bushes or the branches of low apple trees. At last, when nothing seemed to be watching, they went to the nest.

The kingbirds did not plan to go in this roundabout way. They took it because of an instinct that helped them protect their little ones. If Crown and his mate had not gone in a roundabout way, crows and other birds that rob nests could have followed them easily. But no one could find the nest by following Crown and his mate into bushes or apple trees that were far from their home.

The old kingbirds did more than this to protect their young ones. Every time a jay or crow came into their territory, they quickly drove it away. Crown would dash at a crow, fly over its back, and dart down to pull its feathers. Soon his mate would come, too, and would attack the crow. They made such a fuss that the big black bird was glad to get away.

Not all birds are such good fighters as kingbirds, but many kinds defend their nests and young ones. Robins sometimes fly at cats or hungry red squirrels, screaming and beating the beasts with their wings. Catbirds and thrashers peck at snakes that try

93

to eat their eggs or nestlings. Wild geese beat foxes with their wings and strike them with their beaks. Horned owls, which are large, fierce birds, attack beasts and even human beings who try to rob their nests.

Other birds protect their young in very different ways. Bob-whites act as if they were hurt and flutter away from the place where their little ones are hiding. Mother killdeer do this too, dragging themselves over the ground as if they were badly hurt. Cats and foxes follow the mother killdeer, which go farther and farther away from their young ones.

Song sparrows do not pretend to be hurt, and they are too small to attack foxes or cats. Parent birds hide their young ones under bushes or among tall weeds and grass. Then, when a cat or dog comes near, Mother or Father Sparrow says *Tuck! Tuck!* in a loud, sharp tone. That tells the little birds to keep quiet until the danger has passed.

Many water birds hide their young ones and then swim or fly away. Sponsa, the wood duck, does this. So does the mother coot, or mudhen, a gray bird that has a white beak. Young coots can swim soon after they hatch, and they like to follow their parents. But when one of the old birds gives the signal that means "hide," the little ones stay among cat-tails or tall marsh grass, where they cannot be seen.

. . . .

Grown birds also have to protect themselves against dangers of various kinds. Birds that are not as quick and brave as Crown are sometimes attacked by small, long-tailed hawks with brown or gray backs. Woodpeckers escape these hawks by dodging round and round tree trunks. Sparrows and warblers dart into bushes where the hawks cannot go.

Birds that live on the ground, like bobwhites, have to watch out for weasels and cats as well as hawks. Bobwhites hide under bushes when hawks come near, but they run swiftly or fly away from animals that hunt on the ground.

Some birds have powerful weapons which they use to defend themselves. Herons strike with their long, sharp beaks, and many seabirds do so, too. But ostriches, as you know, kick with their long, strong legs and two-toed feet. Since the male ostrich guards the nest, he is the one who drives animals away from the eggs or young ones. He also fights with other male ostriches when they want the same mate.

Coots, often called mudhens, nest beside marshes and swampy lakes. The old birds hide their little ones when danger comes near.

Other Books About Nature and Science

By CARROLL LANE FENTON

Life Long Ago: The Story of Fossils—The tale of "prehistoric" life from primitive sea plants to dinosaurs and Ice Age mammoths.
(Children's Catalog.)

Prehistoric World—Typical animals of the past 350 million years, how they looked, lived, and acted. (ALA *Booklist.*)

Along the Hill—A pocket guide to rocks, minerals, and geology for beginning adults and teen-agers. (ALA *Booklist, Children's Catalog.*)

Earth's Adventures—The story of earth's long and adventurous past, and of the changes that are taking place upon it today. Illustrated by more than 130 drawings and photographs. (ALA *Booklist, Children's Catalog.*)

Along Nature's Highway—The plants and animals to be seen in roadsides and fields. (ALA *Booklist, Children's Catalog.*)

Weejack and His Neighbors—The stories of wild creatures that live on prairies of Canada and the United States. (ALA *Booklist.*)

Wild Folk at the Pond—Animal life in ponds and the small streams that flow into them. (ALA *Booklist, Children's Catalog.*)

Wild Folk in the Woods—"The kind of book . . . which the youngest child can listen to with profit and pleasure."
—*Charleston Evening Post.* (ALA *Booklist.*)

By CARROLL LANE FENTON *and* MILDRED ADAMS FENTON

Worlds in the Sky—"Scientific data, presented with graphic simplicity, highlight the pageantry of the sky."
—*Grade Teacher.* (ALA *Booklist, Children's Catalog.*)

Riches from the Earth—"An excellent book . . . about the rare and everyday riches that come from rocks in the earth." *(Children's Activities.)*